Strategies

for

Teaching

Differently

**CORWIN
PRESS**

The Corwin Press logo—a raven striding across an open book—represents the happy union of courage and learning. We are a professional-level publisher of books and journals for K–12 educators, and we are committed to creating and providing resources that embody these qualities. Corwin's motto is "Success for All Learners."

Strategies for Teaching Differently

ON THE BLOCK
OR NOT

Donna E. Walker

CORWIN PRESS, INC.
A Sage Publications Company
Thousand Oaks, California

For information:

Corwin Press, Inc.
A Sage Publications Company
2455 Teller Road
Thousand Oaks, California 91320
E-mail: order@corwinpress.com

SAGE Publications Ltd.
6 Bonhill Street
London EC2A 4PU
United Kingdom

SAGE Publications India Pvt. Ltd.
M-32 Market
Greater Kailash I
New Delhi 110 048 India

Printed in the United States of America

Library of Congress Cataloging-in-Publication Data

Walker, Donna E.
    Strategies for teaching differently: on the block or not / by Donna E. Walker.
        p. cm.
    Includes bibliographical references.
    ISBN 0-8039-6736-5 (cloth: acid-free paper)
    ISBN 0-8039-6737-3 (pbk.: acid-free paper)
    1. Active learning—United States. 2. Learning, Psychology of. 3. Teaching—United States. 4. Team learning approach in education—United States. 5. Educational change—United States. I. Title.
LB1027.23 .W35 1998
    371.3—ddc21   98-8972

This book is printed on acid-free paper.

98 99 00 01 02 03 10 9 8 7 6 5 4 3 2 1

Production Editor: Sherrise M. Purdum
Editorial Assistant: Kristen L. Gibson
Editorial Assistant: Karen Wiley
Typesetter/Designer: Marion Warren
Cover Designer: Tracy Miller

Contents

Preface

This book is written for every teacher who has hoped for a class where students were actively involved in the learning, where the teacher was the colearner and facilitator, and where there was a collaborative nurturing atmosphere that facilitated high achievement for everyone. Unlike so many books on the market today, this book is not about rhetoric on change but about how to make change happen now.

The uniqueness of this model is that it is systemic rather than piecemeal. One of the reasons that models of the past have failed is that they either addressed only a portion of the needs of change or they mandated reforms for change. When interviewed by J. O'Neil (1995) for *Educational Leadership,* Sizer said, "Mandating reform is like demanding that a Model A Ford go 60 miles per hour without considering that the entire vehicle would need to be overhauled for the speed to change" (p. 12). Most of the books on the market address interesting activities to be used in the classroom but lack a systemic plan for using them. Thus, teachers are left with disjointed activities that the they must try to fit into the lessons. These chapters are about a different approach to teaching and learning.

This book represents years of research on the factors that encourage learning and the factors that impede learning, whether the class is 45 minutes in length or lasts for several hours. In a classroom where quality learning is taking place, a set of characteristics is present. I call this type of quality learning environment *strategic learning* because it follows a specific plan (strategy) and has as its goal quality learning that leads to long-term memory. In a strategic-learning classroom, students are taught in an environment conducive to maximum learning. They are taught meaningful, relevant information that connects to their world and the world in which they will live as adults. Although lecture has its place in some lessons, it should only be used in short segments of time—15 minutes or less. It is unrealistic to believe that students who are constantly stimulated by the multimedia world will sit for hours each day passively listening to lectures, taking notes, and preparing for the pencil-and-paper exam on Friday—all this without dropping out mentally. Life is not a spectator sport, it is an exercise in active involvement: Education should reflect that active involvement. *Breaking Ranks,* the report of the National Association of Secondary School Principals (1996), echoes this belief: "When possible, students should take an active role in their learning rather than as passive recipients of information passed on by textbooks and by teachers who do little more than lecture" (p. 15).

For 6 years, I was involved in a dynamic research project that examined the factors that enhance learning and why they did so. The results of that study are dramatic and touch at the heart of how schools should teach. The project school was transformed into a place of strategic learning. Within 2 years, the results were dramatic. The dropout rate went from 7.4% before implementation to 2.2% at the 2-year mark—and today, shows a dropout rate of 0%. Attendance rates increased by almost 4%. Scholastic Aptitude Test scores zoomed to well above state and national averages and, what is more, students and teachers wanted to go to school each day. In a statistical study of the students over time, it was found that reading and mathematics scores for both males and females rose significantly. All of this was accomplished in a school district where more than 50% of the population qualified for free or reduced-cost lunches under the national poverty standards.

This book is divided into six chapters. Chapter 1 talks about how and why we must move from the structures of the past to a new way of teaching that better prepares students for the 21st century. Chapters 2 and 3 relate to climate. The chapters on climate are so important that without them, the information from the other chapters is powerless.

Chapter 4 deals with the components needed to deliver instruction to students without lectures. This section begins the components of the *learning cycle*. The learning cycle is different from the old lesson cycle because, unlike the lesson cycle, the emphasis in the learning cycle is on the student—where it belongs. Chapter 5 discusses how to ensure that students understand the information studied by requiring that they demonstrate the learning in some way. The last section, Chapter 6, provides the real-world connection to the learning. There are five components to the learning cycle. All five components are not intended to be accomplished in one class period. However, at some point during the unit of study, all five components should be covered. The goal is not only to help students learn but to help them put the information into long-term memory.

This is a very different type of classroom from the one most often found in schools, where teachers are the imparters of knowledge in a lecture format while students memorize facts to give back on paper-and-pencil tests. The transformation takes time and commitment, but it is worth it because it is better for kids.

About the Author

Donna E. Walker is Assistant Superintendent for Curriculum and Instruction for the Allen Independent School District in Allen, Texas. She holds an EdD degree and has 20 years of experience as a classroom teacher, administrator, and innovator in education. She has presented at over 40 national, state, and local meetings. Her research on how children learn and the blocks that prevent student success and the learning strategies she subsequently developed have led to national recognition and this book *Strategies for Teaching Differently: On the Block or Not* (in press). Walker is also the author of *Authentic Teaching and Learning: Anything but Lecture*, which was published in the November 1997 issue of the magazine for Texas Secondary School Principals. She has also served as a principal in an alternative school, as a public relations director, and as a director of finance.

This book is dedicated to my parents,
Jack and Jacqueline Walker, who have
always believed that their children
can accomplish anything.

1

Leaving Lecture Behind

The world we have created is a product
of our thinking; it cannot be changed
without changing our thinking.

—*Albert Einstein*

Throughout the country, schools have raced to block scheduling only to discover that students cannot be taught in the old passive methods of lecture, taking notes, and so forth, in large blocks of time. As we approach a new century, we are still getting the cart before the horse.

In the pilot school for this book, teachers were trained on how to teach students for longer periods of time and without using lecture before the district moved to block scheduling.

Less than 30% of the students in classrooms learn by lecture. If we add to that factor the longer periods of time in class for block scheduling, it is not surprising that students and teachers are frustrated. At the high school level, lecture should be limited to 15 minutes at a time; after that, we lose the majority of the class to daydreaming or disruptive behavior. The strategies in this book have been field tested for 6 years and have been found to provide a dynamic influence on student achievement. The pilot school for this program enjoys high test scores, a low failure rate of less than 4%, and a high attendance rate. Because students are actively involved in the learning all day, few discipline problems exist.

As stated earlier, I call this type of quality learning *strategic learning* because it follows a strategy that is built on meaningful learning. In a strategic classroom, the following characteristics are present:

1. There is a high level of support for achievement. Teachers and students not only expect quality work, they will not accept anything less.

2. Students are given a rubric up front, before an assignment is made, so that they know what is expected. There is no "gotcha" attitude. Students know what they must do to be successful, and they are given the tools to help make success possible. We usually think of learning in terms of the normal bell curve, where a small number are toward the high end of achievement and a small number are at the low end, with the majority in the middle, or "average." The bell curve assumes that some will fail and some will excel but most will be mediocre. That has never been acceptable to me. If students are coming to school and are doing their best and there is still a bell curve, something is wrong with the system. The bell curve should occur before intervention, not after. If teaching follows the principles of strategic learning, there will be a j-curve. In a school with a j-curve of learning, there will be a small number at the bottom and a small number at the center, with the majority at the top. That is what happened in the pilot school. When all students began to learn at a quality level, the overall failure rate dropped to below 4%—a j-curve.

3. Higher-order thinking is emphasized for everyone. Students are given meaningful, challenging work. It is an insult to give students mounds of dittos to complete to fill up time. "Time on task" is important only if the task is meaningful. In an article for *Phi Delta Kappan* on how to improve schools, Gough (1988) quoted Glasser, who said,

> If half of all students are not working because they perceive that school will not satisfy their needs, we have to attend to the fact that a major institution in our society—perhaps the one on which we spend the most money—follows a theory that does not address itself to the needs of more than half of its clients. (p. 656)

In a strategic-learning classroom, the quality of the task is important.

4. There is an emphasis on depth of learning—rather than just covering a great deal of material. Students are given sufficient time and resources to make the learning a part of long-term memory. *Breaking Ranks,* the report of the National Association of Secondary School Principals (NASSP, 1996) says,

> The currently dominant subject-oriented approach to the curriculum leads to an obsessive desire to cram in as much about each subject as possible. Students end up skimming across the surface of a vast curriculum, leaving insufficient time to gain deep, significant understanding. They barely get wet as they swim hurriedly through an ocean of material. (p. 14)

We should truly teach less so that we can teach more.

5. Connections are made to the real world and between the learning. Most students can be taught anything as long as it is relevant to their world. Glasser (as cited in Gough, 1988) says that is why young children learn one of the most difficult things to learn, and learn it without flash cards—they learn a language. One of my favorite math teachers has a sign in her room that should be in every classroom in the United States. It says, "I promise I will never teach you anything in this classroom unless I can tell you how you are going to use it in the real world."

6. The classroom emphasizes collaboration and dialogue. To be successful in the job market, students must be able to articulate what they know and listen to the ideas and opinions of others. Students practice cooperative-learning strategies to help solidify what they have learned and to practice the learning so that when it is time for individual assessment, the learning is in long-term memory. Sizer (1992) says,

> The real world demands collaboration, the collective solving of problems. . . . Learning to get along, to function effectively in a group is essential. Evidence and experience also strongly suggest that an individual's personal learning is enhanced by collaborative effort. The act of sharing ideas, of having to put one's own views clearly to others, of finding defensible compromises and conclusions, is in itself educative. (p. 118)

7. Assessment is a natural progression of the lesson, not something that is tacked on at the end to provide grades for the grade book. David Lazear (1994) says that in the new assessment paradigm, "the lines between the curriculum and assessment are blurred; that is, assessment is always occurring in and through the curriculum and daily instruction" (p. 5). Students are told up front, before the lesson begins, what they must do to demonstrate success. The lines between the goals of the lesson and the assessment are blurred.

8. The environment in the classroom is collaborative and supportive. Glasser (as quoted in Gough, 1988) said,

> Except for those who live in deepest poverty, the psychological needs—love, power, freedom, and fun—take precedence over the survival needs, which most of us are able to satisfy. All our lives, we search for ways to satisfy our needs for love, belonging, caring, sharing, and cooperation. If a student feels no sense of belonging in school, no sense of being involved in caring and concern, that child will pay little attention to academic subjects. (p. 658)

Climate is so important that none of the other techniques discussed will be really effective unless the issue of climate is settled first. In a world full of broken relationships, strong, supportive relationships are important to students. We cannot control the students' environment outside of the classroom, but for 7 hours each day, we have a great deal of control over their environment. It may be our best chance to make the world a better place.

9. Teaching for long-term memory is critical. After years of research on the factors that help students learn and remember as well as the factors that prevent understanding and retention, a model for teaching has emerged that is called, appropriately, the *learning cycle*. It is called the learning cycle because the emphasis is on student learning—where it belongs. Figure 1.1 is a graphic representation of this cycle.

The lesson begins as soon as students enter the room, with a technique that I have labeled *mindjogs*. Mindjogs are based on brain research on how students learn. Like Lazear's (1994) "awakenings," they prepare the students for the lesson. Mindjogs are much like the sponge activities of the past but with a twist—all mindjogs are high level and require complex levels of thought by the student. They also emphasize high interest and take into consideration the students' love of games. These activities are on the board, overhead, or computer or are handed to students as they walk into the room. Their purpose is to jog the mind and prepare the student for the mental workout ahead.

Personal connection is the most critical part of the lesson for those students who have experienced failure in school. The brain research behind this under-standing is powerful. Thanks to the use of magnetic resonance imaging (MRI), we now know that the brain is a seeker of connections. When new information is given to students, chaos in the brain may take place until a connection or hook is made. Unfortunately, for some students, the connection is never made, and years of frustration and failure follow. Personal connection is the part of the lesson that provides a hook for the new learning. Caine and Caine (1991) discussed the brain's need for connections in their book, *Making Connections:* "Our research confirms that the search for meaning is at the heart of intrinsic motivation and that much of the energy and drive to pursue goals and engage in essential tasks comes from the search for meaning" (p. 105). Mindjogs and personal connection are discussed in Chapter 4.

In Chapter 5, information exchange is discussed, and examples are given for ways to teach without lecture. Information exchange is the part of the lesson in which students are given new information. It is the part of the lesson that is most often taught by lecture under the traditional structure. In this model, lecture is limited to 15 minutes—the amount of time that research says we can expect students to listen. Emphasis is placed on depth of learning, not just covering the text. At this stage in the lesson, students are active participants in the learning. They are sharing information and they are practicing the learning together.

Also in this section, we discuss the fourth part of the lesson cycle, informa-tion application. In this part of the lesson, students use the new information in some way, to deepen the understanding and to demonstrate comprehension. Concrete models are emphasized because as many as 60% of the learners in the classroom are usually visual learners.

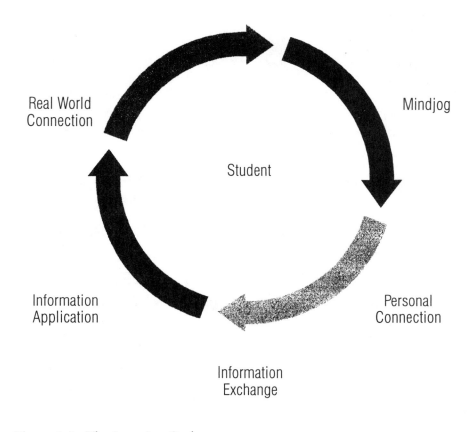

Figure 1.1. The Learning Cycle

Chapter 6 deals with the component of the learning that is critical if students are to apply the learning to their world and put the information into long-term memory. In this part of the lesson, teachers show students how they will use the information in their world. If we cannot tell students how they are going to use the information, why is the information a part of the curriculum? I call this part of the learning cycle *real-world connection.*

The teacher's role in the strategic-learning classroom is critical and is based on these six precepts:

1. Expect that all students can and will achieve at a quality level. James Bellanca and Robin Fogarty (1991), in *Catch Them Thinking,* said, "If and when teachers believe that all students can think and all students need to think, that message is communicated to the students. Teachers who value thinking challenge all students to stretch" (p. 198).

2. Accept only quality work on all student products. Accepting mediocre work is an insult to students and adults alike.

3. Help students understand the meaning, and connect the learning rather than relying on simple drills or exercises to memorize routine facts to pass a test.

4. Serve more as a coach, guide, and facilitator for the students' efforts to learn the material, and ensure that students will be active participants in the learning. "The leader in this role senses when and when not to intercede in the process; she or he is front and center when need arises, but assumes a low profile when the situation seems to be progressing well on its own" (Bellanca & Fogarty, 1991, p. 198.)

5. Provide a variety of assessments that help to give a broad picture of each student's ability and that are directly aligned with the curriculum.

6. Engage students in meaningful work, and incorporate real-world application into the learning.

The strategic-learning classroom is, above all, student centered and follows the challenge to make learning meaningful. This requires a change in the way we view teaching. Many still believe that it is not education that should change but the children who must change. The paradox is that children will not change until we change the way we approach the institution that teaches them. Einstein was right—"We will only change the world when we change our thinking." This book is written in the hope that as we change what we know about teaching, together, we can make learning extraordinary.

Come to the edge, he said. They said: We are afraid.
Come to the edge, he said. They came.
He pushed them . . . and they flew.

—*Apollinaire*

2

Creating a Climate
for Learning

*There is a ceiling effect on how much we can learn if
we keep to ourselves. The ability to collaborate—on
both a small and large scale—is becoming one of the
core requisites of postmodern society. People need
one another to learn and to accomplish things.*

—Michael Fullan (1993, p. 17)

Students, even in small schools, don't know each other unless they happen to be in athletics together or some other organization. As we have talked to students from gangs, one clear message comes through: It is more difficult to hurt someone you know. All students want a sense of belonging—as a matter of fact, belonging is a basic need in all of us. Schools must begin to address the fact that more learning can take place in an environment where there is mutual respect for each other rather than in an environment in which everyone is anonymous. W. Edwards Deming revolutionized the industrial power of Japan by simply showing them how to develop a sense of community within their factories. It is time to revolutionize schools with this same sense of belonging, caring and sharing with one another.

At the beginning of the semester, take time to complete exercises with classes that will help them to get to know each other. The time taken for these activities will be rewarded many times over throughout the semester. Require students to call each other by their first names. Following are four examples of activities to help build a sense of community:

- Name That Name
- Question and Answer Profiles
- A Funny Thing Happened on my Way to
- Find Someone Who

NAME THAT NAME

This is a nonthreatening technique for introducing students at the beginning of the semester. Because we require everyone to be called by their first names or preferred names, this is a good way to help students remember each other. The three steps for this technique are these:

1. Students are grouped into pairs.

2. Students interview each other using the following format:

   - What is your first name?

   - How did you get your name?

   - Is there something unique about your name that will help me remember it?

3. Students introduce each other to the rest of the class.

Variation

Use name tags with information about the student written in each corner, such as favorite sport, music, hobby, class, and so on.

Hobby	Best class
NAME	
Music	Favorite sport

QUESTION AND ANSWER PROFILES

The purpose of question and answer profiles is to help students identify with each other. Team spirit is developed as members find common traits and goals. There are three steps:

1. Students work in groups of two, three, or four.

2. Students share information about themselves with the group.

3. The information is charted to determine likes and differences.

Ask students to look for common interests. A sample chart is shown in Table 2.1.

TABLE 2.1 Question and Answer Profile

Directions: In your study groups, answer the questions below for each individual. Discuss areas where you are alike and areas where you are different as individuals.

Questions	1	2	3
Favorite musical group			
Favorite sport			
In my spare time, I			
My best subject is			
If I could live anywhere, it would be			

A FUNNY THING HAPPENED ON MY WAY TO

There are five steps for this exercise:

1. Students are placed into groups of three or four.

2. Each student briefly shares an experience that relates to the topic given by the teacher.

3. The students decide which experience they will write or tell.

4. All students in the group retell or write about the experience as if it happened to them.

5. A group is called on to tell their experience. The class must guess who really had the experience.

Example:

Read the wonderful book about math anxiety called *Math Curse,* by Jon Scieszka and Lane Smith (1995). Next, ask the question, "Have you ever had trouble learning something important?"

Students share experiences in groups of three or four.

Each group chooses one experience to be their group's experience to share with the class.

The teacher calls on one person from the group to tell the experience. Ask the class to guess who really had the experience.

FIND SOMEONE WHO

This technique has several purposes. It is a great tool for helping students get to know each other, but it is also a meaningful way to learn important information. The three steps are these:

1. Students are given a list of questions.

2. Each student finds other students in the room who can answer each one of the questions. Students initial or write first names by their answers.

3. Students must get a different signature on each question.

Variation:

Use as a review after material has been studied. Instead of personal questions, use questions about the lesson. For example,

Find Someone Who

Knows how to find the area of a polygon _____Length × Width — Margaret

One of the advantages of using this exercise is that once a student finds an answer from another student, he or she becomes an expert on that question and can sign someone else's paper. Those students who never seem to know the answers are elevated to experts.

Table 2.2 shows an example used to help students get to know each other and to determine common interests.

TABLE 2.2 Find Someone Who

Directions: Ask a different person to sign for each of the following.

Find someone who

Likes the same sport as you _____ Mark (baseball)

Has a blue car _____ Marta (Chevy)

Has two brothers _____Rob (ages 8 and 11)

Plans to go to college in another state_____Chris

Had an unusual summer job_____ Jessie (ocean guide)

Plans to become a lawyer_____ Paul

Likes to work with computers _____ Jack

Has a birthday in December _____Kevin (17th)

Has been to Disneyworld _____ Lupe

Has an unusual hobby _____ Dave (taxidermy)

3

Team-Building Strategies

Choice theory teaches that we are all driven by four
psychological needs that are embedded in our genes:
the need to belong, the need for power, the need for
freedom, and the need for fun.

—*William Glasser (1997, p. 599)*

Every one of us wants to belong somewhere. When that need is not satisfied for students in the school setting, they look for it in other places—sometimes, in the wrong places. I was riveted for an entire morning listening to a young man who had been a member of a notorious gang since he was quite young. He was candid about why. He said that he had problems at home and that he didn't fit in with any organization at school (too small for the athletic program, didn't make the cut for gifted, not interested in the academic clubs, etc.) and that the gang offered him a place to belong. Ruby Payne (1996) wrote an article for *The Instructional Leader* in which she eloquently talked about the needs of students from poverty. Her article lists eight resources that these children must have to be successful. Two of those resources are a part of what we are trying to achieve in this chapter. She says that children from poverty need to have strong support systems made up of friends, family, and backup resources and knowledge bases that can be accessed in times of need. She also says that there is a great need for appropriate role models. Perhaps the most impressive of the research that Payne has done points up that

> relationships are the key motivators for learning. For students from
> generational poverty to learn, a significant relationship must be pre-
> sent. When individuals who made it out of poverty are interviewed,

virtually all cite an individual who made a significant difference for them. (p. 3)

I believe that in a world of broken relationships, a sense of belonging is critical to all children, no longer just the children from generational poverty.

To foster this sense of belonging through team building, at the beginning of the semester, a teacher can place the students into study groups of three or four. These study groups stay together for the semester and meet together at least twice each week. The purpose of the study groups is to help each other understand and retain the information being studied and to provide support for learning. Some teachers begin each class with the study groups working together, some end each week with the study groups, some do both. The group is responsible to each other to be sure that work is completed and that everyone understands. After the groups are developed, they may be given more responsibility, such as notifying absent members about homework assignments. Because study groups are teams, the teacher must build that team just as a coach would build an athletic team. The members need to get to know one another, and they must learn to work together in a cohesive manner. This is achieved through team-building activities. Although these activities take time, they pay off in terms of student achievement—and because they tend to cut down on discipline problems, the time is regained many times over. Characteristics of study groups include the following:

- Study groups are made up of three to four students of divergent ability levels.
- The groups meet at least once a week.
- They may begin each class period together to check homework and to be sure everyone understands or to complete a mindjog.

Students are also placed in temporary groups for short-term activities. These groups may be selected by the teacher or by activities that are not only fun but teach as well. Four of the activities that we will discuss include these:

- Trivia Pairs
- Team Name
- Appointments
- Line Up

TRIVIA PAIRS

For this activity, each student is given only part of the information needed. They must find the other person or persons who have the additional information they need. These students make up the group that is to work together for the activity. For example, one student is given the answer to a math equation and two other students are given the parts that make up the equation. These students must find the other students who have the information they need. When the three pieces of information are put together, they form a study group.

Variations:

- Give out a sequence of events on separate slips of paper and have student form groups by putting the events together.

- Give out the name of a country, its climate, location, and products on separate slips of paper and have students form groups by country and its characteristics.

- Pass out titles of songs for students to hum until they find others in the room who are humming the same song.

- Write information or trivia on puzzle parts that must be matched to form the group. For example, *Tora, Tora, Tora* might be written on one puzzle part and *Pearl Harbor* on the other part.

- In various parts of the room, place signs that say *first child, middle child, only child,* and *last child,* and ask students to go the part of the room that describes their birth order. Place students in groups from the four groups.

There are many variations of this exercise. Instead of using personal information, the teacher might use characters from literature and ask students to go to the area of the room that holds a sign naming a character with which they most identify. The teacher might divide the room according to concepts being studied and have students go to the area in which they have the most questions.

TEAM NAME

Study groups who work together over a period of time may give their group a team name. The team names should only be assigned after the team has worked together long enough to know each other. The team name should reflect something about the team. For example, a team might call itself The Number Crunchers because they are very good at putting numbers together in some way or at working problems. Once the group has arrived at a name, the name should be used when referring to the collective group or on papers turned in by the group so that you acknowledge the group's identity.

A variation of this technique is called Bumper Stickers. For this activity, the group comes up with a bumper sticker that reflects their team spirit. Again, the bumper stickers should be used in some way to solidify the identity of the group.

APPOINTMENTS

One of my favorite methods of putting students into temporary groups for an activity is called Appointments and very much reflects the way we work in the business world. This is a good technique when you want students to work with many different students for short periods of time, for example, to review techniques studied or for problem solving. The following three steps should be followed:

1. Give each student a picture of the face of a clock (see Figure 3.1).

2. Each student sets appointments with other students in the classroom. Students put their first name by the appointment time.

3. When the teacher calls out an appointment time, students work with the person who has signed up for that appointment time.

In the illustration shown, if the teacher said, "Go to your 4 o'clock appointment," the student would work with Ryan.

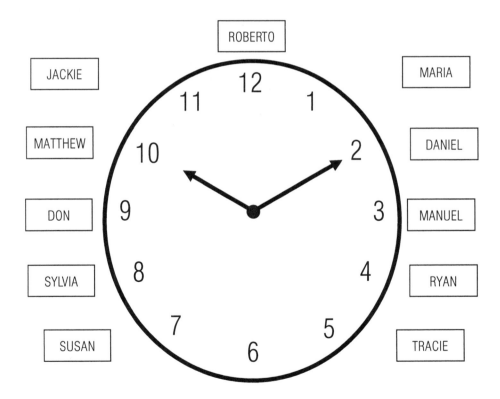

Figure 3.1. Appointments

LINE UP

A quick and easy way to put students into temporary groups is called Line Up. This method is limited only by our imagination in ways to ask students to line up. Some examples to get you started include the following:

Line up by

- The beginning letter of your last name

- Your shoe size

- How you feel about something—such as a school rule or item in the newspaper

- How well you understand a concept

- Your birthday, beginning with January 1

- The number of people in your immediate family

- Answers to math problems, from lowest to highest

- Your favorite literature characters

- Your birth order—first child, middle child, only child, last child

- Where you were born, from farthest away to the closest

After students line up, place them in groups of three or four by having them count off or fold the line over so that students are facing each other, and place them in groups of two with the person they are facing. A variation is to ask students to form two circles facing each other, then ask the outside circle to move three people to the right and place students in groups with the person they are facing.

Constructing Knowledge

Upon the teachers in all high schools falls the responsibility for ensuring that the work that confronts students has the potential to engage them. Even difficult work need not be boring and inaccessible.

—NASSP (1996)

Once the climate has been established in the classroom and study groups have been formed, the teacher is ready to help students expand their knowledge.

In the lesson cycle of the past, the emphasis was on the teacher. I believe the emphasis should be on the student, instead. Current research magnifies this idea, and if we follow best practices in the field, a new model emerges. I call this model the *learning cycle* (see Figure 1.1) because the emphasis is where it belongs—on the student. There are five elements to the learning cycle; the first two will be discussed in depth in this chapter.

Mindjog: Part 1 of the Learning Cycle

Albert Einstein said, "Imagination is more important than knowledge, for knowledge is limited, whereas imagination encompasses the whole world."

As I mentioned briefly in Chapter 1, the first step in this learning cycle is called a mindjog (see Figure 4.1), and its purpose is to jog the mind to prepare for the learning. Mindjogs are activities that emphasize higher level thinking and creativity. Class begins the moment students walk into the classroom. They begin

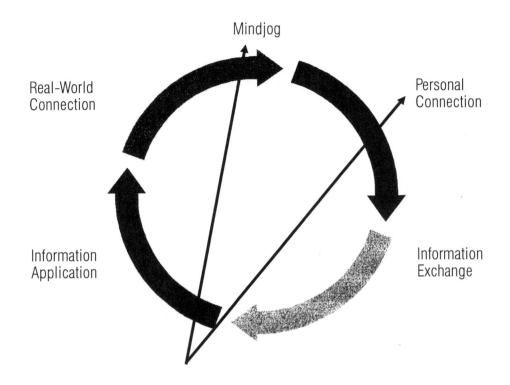

Figure 4.1. The Learning Cycle

with a mindjog activity. The mindjog might be on the overhead, on Powerpoint on the computer, handed to them as they enter the room, or assigned in the previous class. Mindjogs are always high level, interesting, and meaningful. Howard Gardner (1983) calls this the time of "awakening." The brain comes to class asleep and not ready for the level of learning required. Mindjogs awaken the brain and prepare it for the mental workout. Two examples in this chapter are

- Mission Possible
- Where Are You?

Three of our top agents are suspects in a scam to sell arms to Third World countries.

Two of the agents have been trained to always lie when questioned, whereas the third always tells the truth.

> Agent 1: Agent 1 says he did not sell arms to Third World countries.

> Agent 2: Agent 2 says he is the one who sold the arms to Third World countries.

> Agent 3: Agent 3 says that Agent 2 did not sell arms to Third World countries.

Your mission, should you decide to take it (and I know you will), is to find which of the three agents sold the arms to Third World countries. Be able to prove your answer.

Answer: Agent 1. Because Agent 2 and Agent 3 contradict each other, one of them must be telling the truth. Because either Agent 1 or Agent 2 is the only truth teller, Agent 1 must be a liar. Therefore, Agent 1 is the seller.

I like this activity because it is a good introduction to solving for an unknown and to problem solving.

WHERE ARE YOU?

Directions: From the clues given, can you guess "Where are you?"

- Sitting Bull is buried in this state. Where are you?

- Teachers: Produce pictures of geographical places such as Mount Rushmore for students to determine the name of the monument and the location.

- Jefferson is 60 feet tall. Name the state and the place.

Personal Connection: Part 2 of the Learning Cycle

Thanks to brain research and the use of fMRI, we now know that the brain is a seeker of connections. When new information is given to us without any connection in the brain, there is chaos until a connection is made. Sometimes, this is referred to as a schema or framework for the brain. We make assumptions that are often false about what students already know. In her book, *Strengthening Student Learning by Applying the Latest Research on the Brain to Your Classroom,* Marty Sorgen (1995) says, "Without appropriate schema, trying to understand a story, textbook, or classroom lesson is like finding your way through a new town without a map." (p. 5).

Ask: "What do students already know?" What existing frameworks do they already have? If I do not understand that the underlying principle behind algebra is solving for an unknown, I will experience confusion as the teacher moves through the lesson using symbols such as x and y.

Students are not simply passive receivers waiting to be supplied with the correct information; they come to tasks with their own knowledge and expectations. Distortions in recall often occur when new information doesn't fit in an existing schema. We "forget" or distort aspects that are incompatible with our schemas.

Ask: "What misconceptions do my students have?"

The best gift that a teacher can give to those students who traditionally have not done well in school is a hook or framework for the brain so that confusion is eliminated in the brain.

As *Breaking Ranks* (NASSP, 1996) reminds us, "Too often, young people do not recognize connections between events in their everyday lives and what schools teach them. They cannot see the links between what they already know and what they are being taught" (p. 26).

Techniques we will explore include

- KWL
- Group Memory
- Using a Matrix (1)
- Making Predictions
- Before and After

KWL

| *Know* | *Want to know* | *Learned* |

Before the lesson, the teacher uses direct questioning to determine what students know about the content from prior instruction and personal experiences. The teacher may guide the students to categorize the information they have generated. This is an opportunity to correct misconceptions students may have about the information to be studied. This technique may also be used to build interest in the topic.

Next, the students think about what they *want* to learn. They fill in questions they have about what they are about to study. Teachers may want to take the lists from each group and combine them into a class list. The list should be displayed so that the class may refer to it throughout the lesson.

After the lesson, the students evaluate what they have *learned.* This is also an opportunity for the teacher to evaluate whether the lesson has answered student questions and misconceptions.

See Table 4.1 for a sample chart layout for this activity.

TABLE 4.1 KWL

Know	*Want to Know*	*Learned*

GROUP MEMORY

For this activity, students are placed into groups of three. The teacher assigns the topic and gives students the following six-step directions:

1. Write everything you know about the topic.

2. Discuss what you have written with your group.

3. List individual questions that you have about the subject.

4. Share the information with the group. You may write down anything you hear.

5. Compile group questions. Share with the class. A class list should be posted on chart paper or on the board.

6. After the lesson, check questions that were posted earlier.

Suggestions for Use:

- Prior to a study of a historical event, such as the Boston Tea Party

- Prior to a study in science, such as heredity

- Prior to a lesson in math on quadrilaterals

- Prior to a lesson in literature on *Hiroshima,* by John Hersey (1985), ask, "What do you know about the atomic bomb used in World War II?"

Reasons for Using

- Helps to clarify what students know

- Gives the teacher an opportunity to correct false information

- Enhances collaborative skills

- Ties the learning to prior knowledge and to prior questions

USING A MATRIX (1)

This activity is an extension of brainstorming and helps students to think "out of the box." The teacher announces the topic, and students are asked to brainstorm within their groups. Next, students are asked to put their answers into categories.

Suggestions for Use

This technique can be used in any phase of the lesson. In the personal connection phase of the lesson, it is used to help students identify with the new knowledge they are about to receive. For example, before a study on hunger, ask students to brainstorm reasons they believe hunger is a problem in the United States. Next, ask them to plot the information on a matrix in categories such as political reasons, social reasons, economic reasons, and so forth.

Because students often brainstorm ideas that are similar, they can be asked to combine their answers into categories. The teacher should provide the categories until students are very adept at this skill—then, they may form their own categories.

Reasons for Using

- Helps students see information from various points of view

- Enhances the learning for visual learners

- Develops higher-level thinking skills

- Teaches analysis

See Table 4.2 for an example.

TABLE 4.2 Matrix (1)

	Political	*Economic*	*Social*
Urban areas			
Suburban areas			
Intercity			
Rural areas			

MAKING PREDICTIONS

Comprehension is affected by anticipation. Teachers can do a great deal to set the stage for expecting and predicting meaning.

The three-step process for group prediction activities follows:

1. In their study groups, the students read aloud the title of the lesson and several paragraphs about the lesson.

2. The teacher identifies a place in the reading or lesson for predictions.

3. Students work with a partner to predict what will happen next.

Suggestions for Use

Groups make written predications about the lesson based on questions given by the teacher.

For example, for the short story *After Twenty Years*, by O. Henry, the teacher might read the opening paragraphs and ask the class to discuss with a partner what kinds of questions they might ask of each other if they met again after 20 years.

In science class, students might read the background information on a new unit and make predictions about the experiments they will perform.

In math class, students make predictions about how to solve the problems studied.

Reasons for Using

- To arouse curiosity and to make the learning more meaningful
- To heighten awareness of the process

BEFORE AND AFTER

The Before and After exercise is another version of Making Predictions. In this exercise, students must follow up their predictions to determine if their prior knowledge was correct. See Table 4.3 for an example.

TABLE 4.3 Before and After

Directions: Before reading, place a T *in the before-reading column if you believe the statement is true; place an* F *in the column if you believe the statement is false. After you have finished the unit, check to see if your answers were correct.*

Before Reading   After Reading

		1. World War II began with the invasion of Poland.
		2. The Axis Powers were Germany, Italy, and France.
		3. The Soviet Union signed a treaty with Hitler but entered the war on the side of the Allies.
		4. The United States entered the war at its beginning.
		5. The defeated countries were given less punitive punishment at the end of World War II than at the end of World War I.

Answers: 1, 3, and 5 are true; 2 and 4 are false.

Information Exchange: Part 3 of the Learning Cycle

"In brain-based learning, educators see learners as active participants in the learning process. The teacher is not the deliverer of knowledge, but the facilitator and intelligent guide who engages student interest in learning" (Caine & Caine, 1997, p. 87).

Information exchange is the teaching of the lesson with a minimum of lecture. It follows the premises outlined in *Breaking Ranks: Changing an American Institution,* the report of the NASSP (1996). Information exchange emphasizes a curriculum of substance in which

- Students are required to do serious work.
- Instructional strategies that engage students and make them part of the learning process are the rule, not the exception.
- There is a climate supportive of teaching and learning.
- Technology is a part of the teaching and learning and goes far beyond drill and practice.
- Learning is brain based.
- Multiple resources are used.
- Lecture is limited to 15 minutes.
- Collaboration is encouraged.

Techniques we will discuss include

- Bookends
- Think, Pair, Share
- Pairs to Squares
- Expert Groups
- Numbered Heads Together
- Scavenger Hunt
- Six Thinking Hats

As we construct knowledge, it is important to know some of the research behind the idea of students working in teams. If the following statistics, often attributed to William Glasser, are true, they make a good beginning:

We learn

- 10% of what we read
- 20% of what we hear
- 30% of what we see

- 50% of what we see and hear
- 70% of what we discuss with others
- 80% of what we experience personally
- 95% of what we teach others

What are the implications for the traditional lecture approach to teaching?

If we, as teachers, learned our subject best when we began teaching it, what is the implication for allowing students to work together to teach each other, to share information, and to practice the learning?

What is the implication of memorizing facts for a test and then forgetting them afterward as opposed to making the learning meaningful so that students will not forget?

BOOKENDS

Bookends is a technique from cooperative learning that is a good beginning place for those teachers who are reluctant to give up lectures. It incorporates short lecture segments with frequent breaks for students to assimilate the information.

The directions are these six steps:

1. Students focus on the teacher.

2. The teacher gives information to the class for 15 minutes or less.

3. The students discuss the information in pairs.

4. The teacher gives the students additional information for 15 minutes or less.

5. The students discuss the new information.

6. The teacher assigns a task for the class.

Suggestions for Use

- Any time new information is being introduced

- To help break down complex information

Reasons for Using

- To help students assimilate new information

- To teach students to teach information to each other so that the information is internalized

THINK, PAIR, SHARE

This is another cooperative learning technique that helps students give meaning to the information they receive

Directions:

1. Students listen while the teacher poses a question.

2. Students are given time to think of a response. (Variation: Students write a response.)

3. Students turn to a partner and discuss their responses.

4. Groups share their responses with the class.

How to Use

- During those times when you want to give a great deal of information to the class but you want to do it with a minimum of lecture.

- During class discussion so that all students have an opportunity to participate.

- After a new concept has been introduced, to provide opportunities for clarification.

Example: For the unit on Hunger, the teacher might say, "In this country, we produce enough food for every man, woman, and child in the world to have 2100 calories a day. Why, then, are people hungry?"

1. Students are given time to think of a response.

2. Students would share their ideas with a partner or their study group.

3. Groups would share their ideas with the class.

PAIRS TO SQUARES

Pairs to Squares is a variation of Think, Pair, Share. The two steps are

1. Students discuss problems, write answers to questions, and work on problems in pairs.

2. Pairs turn to another pair (to make a square) to check their answers. If the two sets of answers are not the same, the square must discuss until one answer is agreed on.

How and When to Use

- In any subject where there are many steps involved in the solution

- For creative problem solving

- For making predictions; a consensus would not be necessary here as long as the students could give reasons for their predictions. The purpose would be to foster thinking and reasoning abilities.

- To edit and elaborate writing: Each pair writes and the square edits or elaborates or both.

- To check homework

EXPERT GROUPS

Expert Groups is a variation of the cooperative learning technique called *jigsaw.* The four steps are

1. Groups divide the work or information into smaller chunks according to the number in the group.

2. Each member is assigned one part of the material.

3. Members join members from other groups who have the same assignment and agree on what is important and how to teach the material to their learning group.

4. Experts return to their learning groups to take turns teaching each other on their parts of the assignment.

How and When to Use

• When students have a large amount of material to cover

• When the depth of learning is important

• To break down complicated information into chunks for understanding

Example: After reading the first half of the novel *Lord of the Flies,* students are placed in groups of five. Each person in the group is assigned a different character from the book and is given a list of questions about that character. Questions can include the following:

• What does your character look like?

• How does he feel about the other boys in the group?

• How do they feel about him?

• So far, what is his purpose in the story?

After the students have been given about 20 minutes to look up their answers, they move to their expert groups (made up of other students in the class who have the same character). The expert groups compare notes and compile the best answers to the questions. The experts return to their original study groups to teach the information to the group. The teacher calls on characters to speak to the class about their characters. Because the teacher calls on students randomly, all students must be prepared to be the spokesperson for their expert group. At the allotted time, the spokesperson takes on the role of the character assigned. For example, the group that has been assigned the character of Piggy would say, " My name is Piggy and this is what I think of the other boys with me. . . . "

This is a far better way to help students understand the characters than simply reading the novel and answering questions from a ditto. Remember that the objective is to put the information into long-term memory.

NUMBERED HEADS TOGETHER

This is a great cooperative learning technique because it requires that everyone actively participate. The four steps are these:

1. Students number off 1 through 4.

2. Teacher announces a question and a time limit.

2. Students put their heads together and discuss answers to the question.

4. Teacher calls a number, and students with that number answer for the group.

How and When to Use

- To master basic facts and as a test review

- At the knowledge and comprehension level of Bloom's Taxonomy

- As a group competition

- For assessment: Allow groups to make up their own review questions to be used by the teacher. Give bonus points for well-written questions that stump other groups.

Example: In the book *Math Curse,* by Jon Scieszka and Lane Smith (1995), Mrs. Fibonacci counts like this: 1, 1, 2, 3, 5, 8, 13 . . .

What are the next five numbers in Mrs. Fibonacci's counting system?

1. Students discuss the answer in their groups.

2. The students count off from 1 to 4. The teacher checks to see that all groups have done this.

3. The teacher randomly calls a number, such as "3." All of the students who have been designated as Number 3s stand up. The teacher calls on one of them for the answer.

If the answer is correct, the students sit down and the teacher asks another question. If the answer is incorrect, another student is asked to give the answer. One of the advantages of this technique is that everyone must be alert at all times because no one knows who will be accountable for the answer. Another advantage is that when a student answers, the answer is not only his or her own but the answer of the group, and there is less stigma about getting the answer wrong.

SCAVENGER HUNT: ARE YOU HUNGRY?
A SCAVENGER HUNT ABOUT HUNGER IN THE UNITED STATES

Rules for the hunt:

1. You must work in groups of four, with each member contributing equally to the whole group effort.

2. You can go anywhere that is appropriate to obtain your data. Cameras and tape recorders may be used to record information. Written summaries of television shows, hand-drawn maps, and diagrams are acceptable.

3. Use primary sources when possible.

4. The sources of all data must be recorded.

Items to Collect and Create

1. Collect three to five articles about poverty in the United States. Be sure that they cover more than one category (homelessness, unemployment, overpopulation, etc.)

2. Chart how the United States spends money to help the poor in our country.

3. Collect at least five songs that have the theme of poverty. Share the lyrics in some unique way with the class.

4. On a map of the United States, locate the five areas that contain the largest number of people in poverty. Research the reasons why.

5. Chart a matrix on how overpopulation, hunger, and poverty can affect the environment.

6. Find out the number of homeless and unemployed in your community. Chart or graph your findings.

7. Mindmap the causes of poverty. (A mindmap is a graph that helps the brain make visual connections between thoughts, ideas, words, or pictures.)

8. Create a list of things that individuals can do to help alleviate poverty in their community or their country.

SIX THINKING HATS

Edward DeBono (1985) wrote a wonderful book titled *Six Thinking Hats.* The book was written to help people in business and industry break out of their traditional thinking so that problems and innovations could be approached from a fresh direction. The ideas work well in the classroom, where we so often get "cookie cutter" type ideas from students. Another advantage to using this technique in the classroom is that it is a nonthreatening way to get usually negative-thinking students to think in another direction. Because they are playing a role in the activity, the technique is not threatening.

How to Use in the Classroom

Assign each group in the classroom a different hat. Based on the definition of the hat, the group approaches the assignment only from the viewpoint of the hat they have been given.

For our lesson on Hunger, the assignments might be thus:

Group 1: White Hat Thinking

This group looks only at the facts about hunger in the United States. They are not concerned with "I think or I feel" perspectives, only with data.

Group 2: Red Hat Thinking

This group is concerned with hunches and feelings about the problem of hunger in the United States. These hunches do not have to be backed by hard data. The members will report their opinions about the problem.

Group 3: Black Hat Thinking

This group will report all of the reasons why efforts to end hunger in the United States will not work. Their answers will be based on logic from a negative viewpoint.

Group 4: Yellow Hat Thinking

This group will report all the reasons that efforts to feed the poor will work. They will focus on the benefits of the efforts to end hunger and the constructive thinking that can make it happen.

Group 5: Green Hat Thinking

This group will focus on the innovative ideas that are being considered to end hunger. Their emphasis will be creative, new, and innovative approaches.

Group 6: Blue Hat Thinking

This group will be responsible for the organization of the project. They will manage the other groups to see that they are on target and that they have the tools they need to complete their tasks. This group will also be responsible for the evaluation of the project and for tying all of the thinking together. In the first few projects that I do with this model, as the teacher, I am the blue hat thinker.

The maturity and expertise of your class will determine at what point students are ready to take this role.

Variation

Frames of Reference: Groups are handed picture frames with specific words or ideas written on them, and the groups look at the information to be studied from those viewpoints. For example, the frames might be identified by Who, What, Where, How, and When. In the events leading up to World War II, *Who* were the key players, *What* events were significant, *Where* were the events taking place and what was the significance of the location, *How* were people reacting to the events, and *When* were the critical events taking place?

CHAPTER 5

Demonstrating Understanding

*Learning is an active process in which meaning is
developed on the basis of experience.*

—*Duffey and Jonassen (1992)*

Information Application: Part 4 of the Learning Cycle

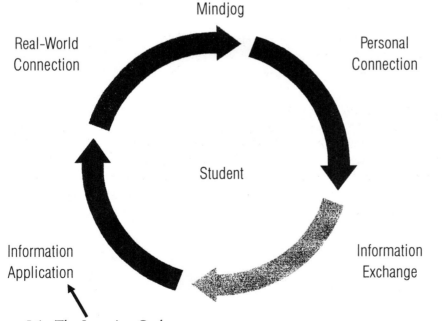

Figure 5.1. The Learning Cycle

At this point in the lesson, students are given the opportunity to demonstrate understanding of the learning by using the information they have learned in some way. Students who learn best by tactile or visual means need the opportunity to use graphic or concrete models to help solidify the information. Concrete models are some of the best gifts that we can give to the learners at this point, particularly the visual learners. The word *concrete* in the title is not by accident—concrete models help to put ideas in concrete for the student.

A variety of concrete models will be demonstrated in this section. They include the following:

- Collaborative Retelling
- Alike and Different
- Fat and Skinny Questions
- Attribute Webs
- Mindmaps
- Thinking at Right Angles
- Using a Matrix
- Fishbone
- Venn Diagrams

Concrete Models

What Are Concrete Models?

Concrete models are visual representatives of the learning. They are mental maps to help students understand and remember difficult concepts, such as sequencing, comparing and contrasting, and classifying.

Why Use Concrete Models?

Concrete models help students connect or relate new information to prior knowledge. Because they make abstract ideas more visible, they help students understand and remember concepts that are difficult to visualize otherwise. Students who are visual learners need concrete models to help them organize and process information.

When Do We Use Concrete Models?

Concrete models can be used at any time during the learning process but are critical in the phase of the lesson in which the teacher wants the students to use the new information in some way. This is a time for clarifying ideas for both the student and the teacher prior to assessment. Other times in which concrete models might be used include

- Introducing a difficult or abstract concept
- Assessing the learning
- Being a part of an individual or group project
- Demonstrating understanding of a concept
- Demonstrating creativity

COLLABORATIVE RETELLING

Collaborative Retelling reinforces the learning by giving students opportunities to repeat the information learned. This is also a technique that encourages elaboration because students are prompted to remember details.

The five steps are as follows:

1. Students are placed into groups of two.

2. The teacher hands out the Collaborative Retelling sheet to each pair of students (see Table 5.1 for an example).

3. Students number off so that there is a Student 1 and a Student 2.

4. Student 1 asks Student 2 to tell everything he or she remembers about the lesson. As ideas are mentioned, Student 1 puts a check mark in the "First Retelling" column.

5. When Student 2 is finished, Student 1 uses clues to help Student 2 remember details not mentioned. Student 1 checks off items student 2 is able to elaborate.

TABLE 5.1 Collaborative Retelling for *After Twenty Years* by O'Henry

First Retelling	Clued Retelling	
		The promise
		The setting
		The lamppost
		The policeman
		The cigarette
		The betrayal

ALIKE AND DIFFERENT

This model can be used for any subject in which students need to make comparisons. Before students can compare, they must understand attributes. This is a beginning step for more difficult comparing and contrasting activities.

At the beginning level, teachers give the categories. As students learn to think in flexible terms, they can add their own categories. See Table 5.2 for an example.

TABLE 5.2 "Alike and Different" Example

CLINTON		DOLE
How Alike?		
How Different With Regard to:		
	Education policy	
	Foreign policy	
	Tax cuts	
	Medicare	

FAT AND SKINNY QUESTIONS

Fat questions require lots of discussion and explanation with interesting examples. Fat questions take time to think through and answer in depth.

Skinny questions require simple yes, no, or maybe answers.

Ways to Use

Ask students to make up five fat questions and five skinny questions about a lesson.

Reasons for Using

- Teaches collaborative skills

- Increases awareness of in-depth questioning

For examples, see Table 5.3.

TABLE 5.3 Fat and Skinny Questions

Directions: In the column for Fat questions, list questions that cannot be answered by "yes" or "no" or with one-word answers. Under the column for Skinny questions, list questions that can be answered with one-word answers.

Fat?	Skinny?
1. What were the events that led to World War II?	1. When did World War II begin?
2. How was Hitler able to rise to power in Germany?	2. When did the United States enter the war?
3. Why didn't the United States enter the war before Pearl Harbor?	3. Who was President of the United States during the war?
4. Compare and contrast Winston Churchill and Franklin D. Roosevelt.	4. Who were the Allies?
5. What were the agreements reached at Yalta?	5. Who attacked the United States at Pearl Harbor?

Brainstorming Models

Brainstorming is a way to get many ideas before the class. The emphasis is on quantity at this point. As the teacher, you will want to encourage all students to participate and to share their ideas on the subject. To encourage this free flow of ideas, rules must be established before the brainstorming session. The teacher must set basic rules for brainstorming. The following is a suggested set:

Rules for Brainstorming

- Accept all ideas without judgment—One person's ideas may lead to other ideas.
- Look for as many ideas as you can—The emphasis is on quantity at this point.
- Make yourself stretch for new ideas—Common ideas are usually repeated first. Wait for a pause in the flow of ideas because the most creative ideas usually come after the pause.
- Seek combinations of ideas and use the ideas of others to expand to new ideas—This is one of those times when using others' ideas is encouraged.

Mindmaps and Attribute Webs, whose descriptions follow, are brainstorming models.

MINDMAPS

Mindmaps are visual pictures of the learning. They provide a way to show a great deal of information in a small space. The main idea is written in the center circle, with subordinating ideas in the smaller circles. Additional ideas about the subordinating ideas are written on the lines that extend from the circles.

Variation

Ask students to prove their information with page numbers from the text or other sources in the subordinating ideas circles (see Figure 5.2).

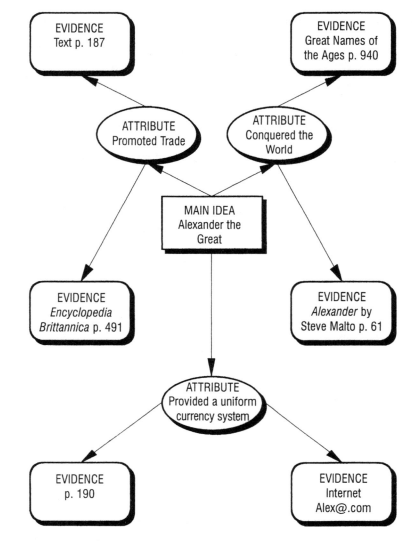

Figure 5.2. A Sample Mindmap

ATTRIBUTE WEBS

An attribute web is a variation of the mindmap. It is a way to show attributes in a concrete form. A web begins with a main idea, and attributes of that idea are placed on the spokes coming from the main idea.

For example, ask students to analyze the attributes of their study of Alexander the Great. The word *heredity* is placed in the center of the web, and the characteristics of heredity are written on the lines extending from the center of the web. This is a good beginning activity for higher-level thinking models, such as comparing and contrasting or for making Venn diagrams.

This is also a good beginning activity for writing reports or for research projects because it requires students to break down a complex topic into smaller parts. See Figure 5.3 for an example.

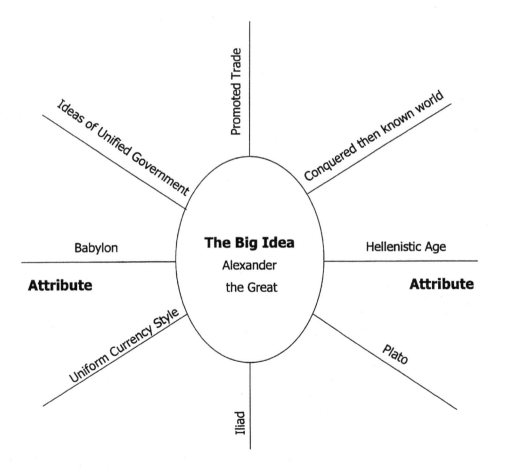

Figure 5.3. A Sample Attribute Web

Thinking in Categories

This section explores ways to help students (a) expand their thinking by looking at information in various ways, (b) approach problems from different directions, and (c) look at information from many points of view. Included in this section are the following activities:

- Thinking at Right Angles
- Using a Matrix
- Fishbone
- Venn Diagrams

THINKING AT RIGHT ANGLES

This activity helps students to associate their ideas and to expand ideas into new categories.

For example: Ask students to list, on the right side of the angle, characteristics of a character they have been studying. On the left arrow, write ideas that come to you as you list characteristics. This might include personal experiences, other people with this characteristic, and so forth.

In Table 5.4, information about the people killed in the Holocaust was given on the horizontal side of the angle. The student wrote his own thoughts about the information in the vertical part of the angle.

TABLE 5.4. Thinking at Right Angles—Example: The Holocaust

Directions: Fill in the mindmap using concrete evidence from your text or other sources.

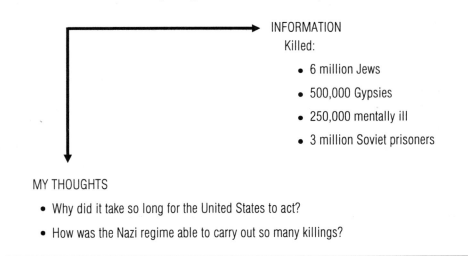

INFORMATION

Killed:

- 6 million Jews
- 500,000 Gypsies
- 250,000 mentally ill
- 3 million Soviet prisoners

MY THOUGHTS

- Why did it take so long for the United States to act?
- How was the Nazi regime able to carry out so many killings?

USING A MATRIX (2)

As mentioned in Chapter 4, using a matrix is a good way to get students to look at information from more than one point of view.

For example: You might give students a matrix with the names of countries studied going down the left column and categories such as population, currency, ethnicity, products, and greatest national problem written across the top cells. Students fill in the cells under the categories for each country.

This activity can be used at any point in the lesson cycle, including evaluation. See Table 5.5 for an example.

TABLE 5.5 Matrix (2)

	Population	Currency	Products	Greatest Problem
Greece				
Italy				
France				
Spain				

FISHBONE

A fishbone can be used when you want students to analyze information or as a first step in problem solving. The problem is written in the box, with each part of the fishbone representing a breakdown of the problem, such as who, what, when, where, how, and why. Students analyze each of the subtopics to determine the cause of the problem.

Variation

Use as a visual representation of causes that lead to an event. For example: Place the words *World War II* in the box, and ask students to list causes in the bones of the fish (see Figure 5.4 for an example).

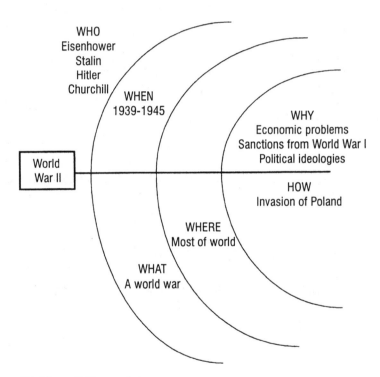

Figure 5.4. "Fishbone" Example

VENN DIAGRAMS

Using Venn diagrams is an excellent way to help students see how things are alike and how they are different. A prerequisite to this kind of thinking is the ability to determine attributes.

For example: Ask students to list attributes they have learned about World War I and World War II. Ask them to plot those ideas on a Venn diagram with the attributes that both share in the center and the individual attributes on the outer edges of the circles (see Figure 5.5 for an example).

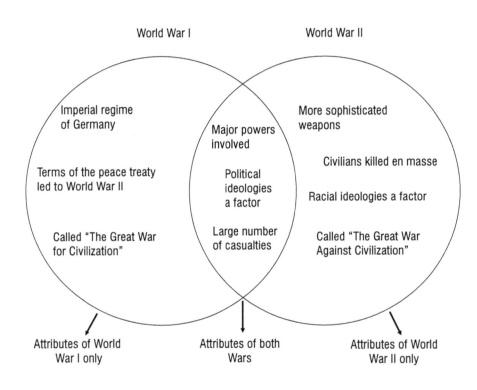

Figure 5.5. Venn Diagram: Compare and Contrast Example

CHAPTER 6

Reflecting on the Learning

Whenever students are being helped to see major concepts, big ideas, principles, and generalizations and not merely engaged in the pursuit of isolated facts, better teaching is going on. A fundamental goal of education is the ability to deal with various and competing ways of understanding the universe. Knowing how to spell is not enough.

—Martin Haberman, (1997, p. 3)

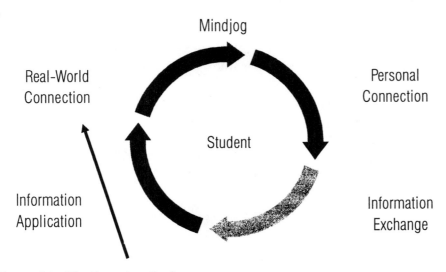

Figure 6.1. The Learning Cycle

Real-World Connection: Part 5 of the Learning Cycle

Real-world connection could be called the "forgotten" part of the lesson. We talk to students about wars of the past, even have them memorize information about those wars, and often never talk to them about the wars that are imminent in their lifetime and strategies they need to know to avoid those wars. Dr. William Glasser (1994) said, "Our curriculum is worthless if we cannot convince students that they are learning useful life skills" (p. 1).

This part of the learning includes these two aspects:

1. Showing students how they are going to use the information in the real world. Example: After the completion of the unit on hunger in the United States, ask students to come up with possible solutions and evaluate those solutions based on feasibility in their world today. Use a matrix or mindmap to display the information.

2. Helping students reflect on the learning. This is a time of metacognition in which students evaluate the learning and its meaning to their world. Example: After a unit on immigration, ask students to graph the problems associated with too many people immigrating to one area. How does immigration affect the quality of life for the receiving country and for the countries from which these people come? What are the solutions? What kinds of decisions will they make in their lifetime that will affect immigration?

Another example: After a unit on slope, ask students to research the rules about slope for wheelchair access to public buildings. Do the buildings in the immediate area meet the standards?

The possibilities are endless. The key question that teachers must ask themselves as they develop units is "What does this have to do with the life my students live now or will live in the future?" At last, we are answering the age-old question students ask: "When are we ever going to use this information?" The answer is now!

Examples follow of four activities that can help bring the information you are teaching into the students' real world:

■ What, So What, Now What
■ Ticket Out the Door
■ PMI
■ Reflections

WHAT, SO WHAT, NOW WHAT

Students answer three questions about the lesson or unit after its completion.

The first question is, " What have I learned?" Students are asked to list key ideas that they learned from the lesson or unit.

The second question is, "So what difference does it make?" Students reflect on why they have learned the information.

The third question is, "Now, what can I do with the learning?" Students reflect on what the new information has to do with their world. This is a guide for both students and teachers about the value of the lesson. The technique could also be used as an assessment of the learning or as a way to begin dialogue about real-world application. See Figure 6.2 for an example.

What (have I learned)?
   I have learned that world hunger is not caused by the lack of food produced but by a multitude of reasons, including transportation, politics, poverty, and a lack of infrastructure to ensure that farmers can survive.

So What (difference does it make)?
   The problem will continue to grow without a workable plan. Because poverty and hunger often force people to harm the environment and others, the problem belongs to all of us.

Now What (can I do with this information)?
   Awareness is the first step toward solving the problem. I must become more active in my own community to help solve the problems of hunger, and as a registered voter, I can make a difference by informed voting about issues that affect food production.

Figure 6.2. What, So What, Now What

TICKET OUT THE DOOR

In this technique, students answer a question individually or in groups about the lesson. The information is given to the teacher when the bell rings as their "ticket out the door." This technique is a great way for teachers to evaluate the effectiveness of the lesson because students who did not understand the lesson will not be able to give in-depth answers. See Figure 6.3 for examples.

I Learned That
   There are many reasons why people leave their countries to immigrate here. Some of the reasons are political, some are economic, some are social, and some are religious in nature.

I Changed my Mind About
   The reasons people immigrate

Because
   I looked at social, economic, political, and religious factors in the countries from which people leave to come to this county.

I Am Confused About
   The discrepancies in immigration policies between states and countries

---

Figure 6.3. Ticket Out the Door

This is a technique originated by Edward DeBono (1985) in which students evaluate the lesson by listing the positive things they have learned in the Plus column, negative feelings in the Minus column, and interesting thoughts or ideas in the Interesting column. The purpose is to guide students to think about what they have learned. See Figure 6.4 for some examples.

Directions: In the chart that follows, list something you have learned in this unit that will be helpful to you in the "Plus" section. List something you still don't understand or something you feel negative about in the "Minus" section. In the "Interesting" section, list something that you observed in the unit or an original idea that you have in regard to the learning.

Plus

The study of World War II demonstrated the power of people in the United States when they focused on the same objective.

Minus

I still believe the United States was slow getting involved.

Interesting

I think we should have a USO Day at our local nursing home and dress up in the clothes of the World War II era. We could provide entertainment music from that era. Many of those in nursing homes today identify with that time—some even fought in the war.

Figure 6.4. PMI (Plus, Minus, and Interesting Observations)

REFLECTIONS

In this variation of Ticket Out the Door, students list three things they have learned and any unanswered questions. See Figure 6.5 for a sample list. This is a good technique to do in the middle of a unit to determine whether students understand the information.

Learned	Unanswered Questions
1. George Washington was born in Virginia and was a farmer.	Why did he refuse to run for a third term?
2. As the commander of the American army during the Revolutionary War, he is remembered for keeping up morale during the hard winter at Valley Forge.	How did the story of the cherry tree get started?
3. Some of the traits that he exhibited are courage, impartiality, and good judgment.	

Figure 6.5. Three Major Learnings

Resource A
Assessing Your School—
How Do You Measure Up?

Directions: Please respond to the questions below by circling the most appropriate number along the continuum line.

1. What is the teaching style in your school?

1	2	3	4	5	6

   Lecture   Active participation

2. What is your major curriculum source?

1	2	3	4	5	6

   Textbook   Multiple sources

3. How are the students involved in their learning?

1	2	3	4	5	6

   Passive   Active

4. What is the role of parents in your school?

1	2	3	4	5	6

   Visitors   Partners

5. What is the role of leadership in your school?

1	2	3	4	5	6

   Authoritarian   Transformational

6. How would you describe communications among
   staff members in your school?

1	2	3	4	5	6

What?   Open

7. What is the quality of staff development in your school?

1	2	3	4	5	6

Spray and pray   Meaningful

8. How are the written, taught, and tested curriculum linked?

1	2	3	4	5	6

Not   Systemic

9. What is the role of students in the learning process?

1	2	3	4	5	6

Passive learners   Active participants

10. What is the climate in your school?

1	2	3	4	5	6

Cloudy with a chance of rain   Clear, with a ray of sunshine

Resource B:
Expanding the Learning—
An Annotated Bibliography

General Information

Barrett, S. L. (1992). *It's all in your head.* Minneapolis, MN: Free Spirit Publishing (400 First Avenue North, Suite 616, 55401, 612/338-2068).

An easy-to-read book about the brain

Bellanca, J., & Fogarty, R. (1991). *Blueprints for thinking in the cooperative classroom.* Palatine, IL: Skylight Publishing (200 W. Wood Street, Suite 250, 60067).

Cooperative learning basics with examples to use in the classroom

Caine, R. N., & Caine, G. (1997). *Education on the edge of possibility.* Alexandria, VA: Association for Supervision and Curriculum Development (1250 N. Pitt Street, 22314-1453, 800/933-2723).

A book about the possibilities in the classroom if we follow brain-compatible learning

National Association of Secondary School Principals. (1996). *Breaking ranks: Changing an American institution.* Reston, VA: Author (1904 Association Drive, 22091-1537, 703/860-0200).

A report on the needs of the high school of the 21st century

Sylwester, R. (1995). *A celebration of neurons: An educator's guide to the human brain.* Alexandria, VA: Association for Supervision and Curriculum Development (1250 N. Pitt Street, 22314-1453, 800/933-2723).

A guide to how the brain works

Mindjogs

McClintock, J., & Helgren, D. (1986). *Everything is somewhere.* New York: William Morrow.

A quiz book on geography and people

Rohrer, D. (1993). *Thought provokers.* Berkeley, CA: Key Curriculum Press (PO Box 2304, 94702, 510/548-2304).

Puzzles for the mind

Rubin, D. (1990). *More brain storms.* New York: HarperCollins.

Ingenious mind puzzles that teach

Personal Connection

Caine, R. N., & Caine, G. (1991). *Making connections.* Alexandria, VA: Association for Supervision and Curriculum Development (1250 N. Pitt Street, 22314-1453, 800/933-2723).

A guide to brain-based learning

Costa, A. (1991). *Developing minds: A resource book for teaching thinking.* Alexandria, VA: Association for Supervision and Curriculum Development (1250 N. Pitt Street, 22314-1453, 800/933-2723).

A good resource for investigating brain research and its application

Information Exchange

Bellanca, J. (1990). *Keep them thinking III.* Palatine, IL: Skylight Publishing (200 W. Wood Street, Suite 250, 60067).

Classroom ideas for getting students involved. Also see *Teach them thinking* by the same author

DeBono, E. (1984). *Six thinking hats.* Boston, MA: Little, Brown.

Helping people think in out-of-the-box terms

Kagan, S. (1992). *Cooperative learning.* San Juan Capistrano, CA: Kagan Cooperative Learning (27134 Paseo Espada, Suite 303, 92675, 800/ 266-7576).

Cooperative learning techniques for group learning

Information Application

Black, H., & Black, S. (1992). *Organizing thinking book II*. Pacific Grove, CA: Midwest Publications (PO Box 448, 93950).

Graphic models for the classroom

Marguilies, N. (1992). *Mapping inner space*. Tucson, AZ: Zephyr Press (3316 North Chapel Ave., 85728-6006, (520) 322-5090).

Teaches how to mindmap

Resource C
Sample Lesson Forms

Blank Sample Lesson Form

Lesson _____

Title of Lesson:

Goals:

Classroom Management:
Groups:
Method:
Roles:
Materials:

The Learning Cycle

Mindjog:

Personal connection

Information exchange:

Information application:

Real-world connection:

Reflections:

Assessment:

Lesson _____

Title of Lesson: The Players at Yalta—World War II

Goals:

To introduce the powers that influenced the Yalta Agreement: Stalin, Roosevelt, and Churchill

Classroom Management:

Groups: 4 groups

Method: Students are given a ticket for a trip to Yalta as they enter the classroom. The tickets are color coded:

Purple—Stalin Group

Green—Churchill Group

Red—Roosevelt Group

Yellow—News reporter

Roles: Leader, Spokesperson, Interpreter, Timekeeper

Materials: Packets that include

- Background information
- Pieces of information about the person their group represents; each person has a different piece of information.
- Rubric
- KWL chart
- Attribute Web
- Find Someone Who

The Learning Cycle

Mindjog: Where Are You? (Clues about Yalta)

Techniques used: Think, Pair, Share; Pairs to Squares

Personal connection: Fill out K of KWL chart, share answers with
group and then with the class. Next, fill out the W of the KWL
chart and share information.

Information exchange: Each student becomes an expert on the piece
of information they have been given in their packets. Together in
their groups they will share attributes about the person they have
been assigned.

Information application: Complete an attribute web about the
person assigned.

Real-world connection: Present information to the class about the
person assigned. Answer questions about his role at Yalta
and how that has affected us today.

Reflections: Find Someone Who (has information about World War II)

Assessment: Rubric on criteria for presentations

Resource D
Blackline Masters

ALIKE AND DIFFERENT

How Alike?

How Different With Regard to:		

APPOINTMENTS

DIRECTIONS: Make appointments with 12 people in the room. Ask each student to initial the time of their appointment to work with you.

ATTRIBUTE WEB

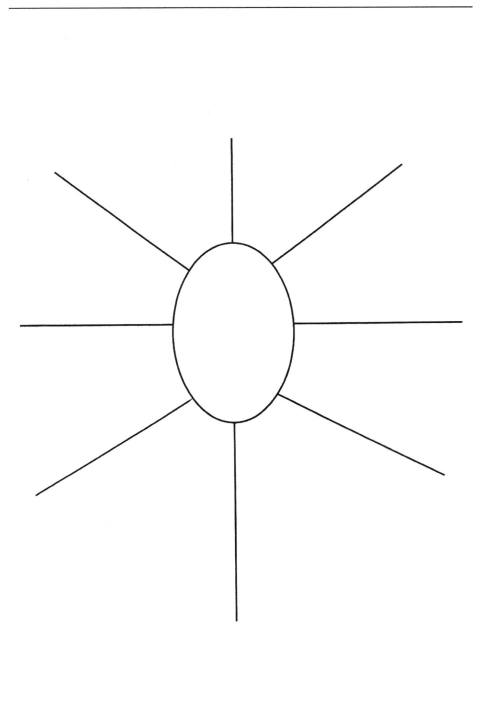

BEFORE AND AFTER

Directions: Before reading, place a T in the before-reading column if you believe the statement is true; place an F in the column if you believe the statement is false. After you have finished the unit, check to see if your answers were correct.

Before Reading   *After Reading*

1.

2.

3.

4.

5.

COLLABORATIVE RETELLING

First Retelling	Clued Retelling	

FAT AND SKINNY QUESTIONS

Directions: In the column for Fat questions, list questions that can not be answered by "yes" or "no" or with one-word answers. Under the column for Skinny questions, list questions that can be answered with one-word answers.

Fat?	*Skinny?*
1.	1.
2.	2.
3.	3.
4.	4.
5.	5.

FIND SOMEONE WHO

Directions: Ask a different person to sign for each of the following:

Find someone who

Likes the same sport as you

Has a blue car

Has two brothers

Plans to go to college in another state

Had an unusual summer job

Plans to become a lawyer

Likes to work with computers

Has a birthday in December

Has been to Disneyworld

Has an unusual hobby

FISHBONE

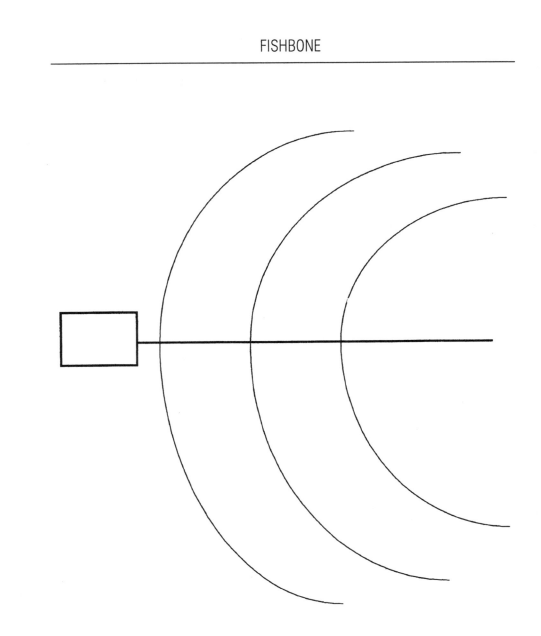

KWL

Know	Want to Know	Learned

MINDMAP

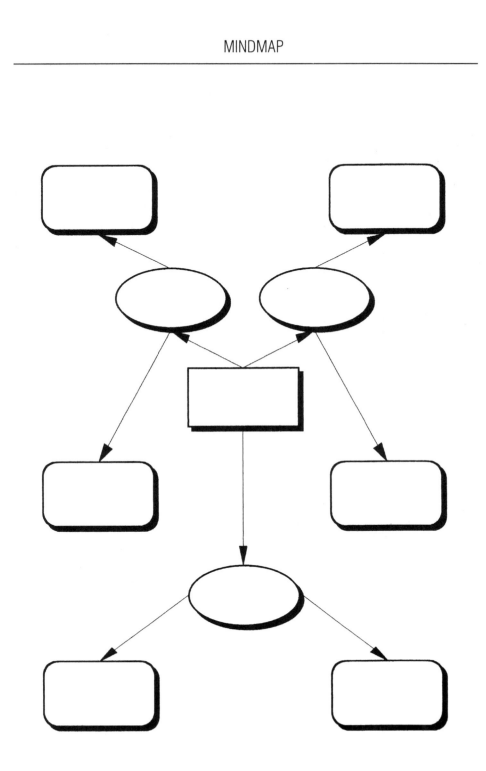

PMI
(Plus, Minus, and Interesting Observations)

*Directions: In the chart that follows, list something you have learned in this
unit that will be helpful to you in the "Plus" section. List something you still don't
understand or something you feel negative about in the "Minus" section.
In the "Interesting Observations" section, list something that you observed in the unit
or an original idea that you have in regard to the learning.*

Plus

Minus

Interesting Observations

QUESTION AND ANSWER PROFILE

Directions: In your study groups, answer the questions below for each individual. Discuss areas where you are alike and areas where you are different as individuals.

Questions	1	2	3

Favorite musical group _____

Favorite sport _____

In my spare time, I _____

My best subject is _____

If I could live anywhere, it would be _____

THINKING AT RIGHT ANGLES

Directions: Fill in the mindmap using concrete evidence from your text or other sources.

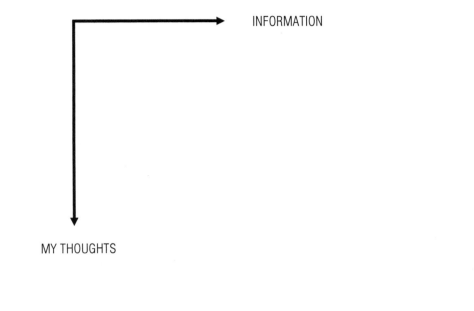

INFORMATION

MY THOUGHTS

THREE MAJOR LEARNINGS

I Learned	*Unanswered Questions*
1.	1.
2.	2.
3.	3.
4.	4.
5.	5.

TICKET OUT THE DOOR

I learned that

I changed my mind about

Because

I am confused about

VENN DIAGRAM
Compare and Contrast

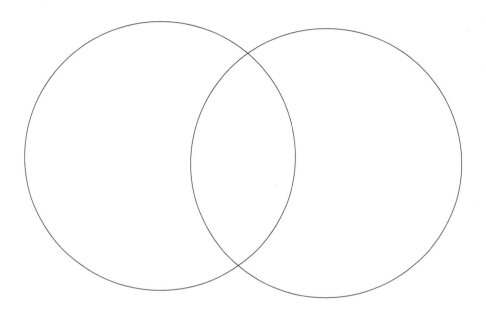

WHAT, SO WHAT, NOW WHAT

What (have I learned)?

So What (difference does it make)?

Now What (can I do with this information)?

References

Bellanca, J., & Fogarty, R. (1991). *Blueprints for thinking in the cooperative classroom.* Palantine, IL: Skylight.

Burke, K. (1992). *What to do with the child who.* Palantine, IL: Skylight.

Caine, R., & Caine, G. (1991). *Making connections: Teaching and the human brain.* Alexandria, VA: Association for Supervision and Curriculum Development.

Caine, R., & Caine, G. (1997). *Education on the edge of possibility.* Alexandria, VA: Association for Supervision and Curriculum Development.

DeBono, E. (1985). *Six thinking hats.* Toronto, Ontario, Canada: Key Porter.

Duffey, J., & Jonassen, D. (1992). *Constructivism and the technology of instruction: A conversation.* Hillsdale, NJ: Lawrence Erlbaum.

Fullan, M. (1993). *Change forces: Probing the depths of educational reform.* Bristol, PA: Fulmer.

Gardner, H. (1983). *Frames of mind.* New York: Basic Books.

Gardner, H. (1993). On teaching for understanding: A conversation with Howard Gardner. *Educational Leadership, 50*(7), 4-7.

Glasser, W. (1994, March/April). Teach students what they will need in life. *ATPE News,* 20-21.

Glasser, W. (1997). A new look at school failure and school success. *Phi Delta Kappan, 78*(8), 599.

Gough, P. B. (1988). The key to improving schools: An interview with William Glasser. *Phi Delta Kappan, 68*(9), 656.

Haberman, M. (1997). What star teaching actually looks like. *Instructional Leader, 10*(1), 3-5.

Hersey, J. (1985). *Hiroshima.* New York: Vintage.

Lazear, D. (1994). *Multiple intelligence approaches to assessment.* Tucson, AZ: Zephyr.

National Association of Secondary School Principals. (1996). *Breaking ranks: Changing an American institution.* Reston, VA: Author.

O'Neil, J. (1995). On lasting school reform: A conversation with Ted Sizer. *Educational Leadership, 52*(5), 12.

Payne, R. (1996). Understanding and working with students and adults from poverty. *The Instructional Leader, 9*(2), 3.

Scieszka, J., & Smith, L. (1995). *Math curse.* New York: Viking.

Sizer, T. (1992). *Horace's school: Redesigning the American high school.* Boston: Houghton Mifflin.

Sorgen, M. (1995). *Strengthening student learning by applying the latest research on the brain to your classroom.* Bellevue, WA: Bureau of Education and Research.